Written by Patricia Gray
Illustrated by Martina Selway

Longman

If anyone tells you
"You are as clumsy as an elephant!"
tell them an elephant is not
clumsy at all. It is really
very careful and sure-footed.

The African elephant is the biggest
and strongest land animal in the
world. Yet it can move about and
scarcely make a sound with its
great padded feet.

The elephant likes to live in a herd. It is miserable when it is on its own.

The herd moves a long way each day
in search of food. An elephant
eats leaves, roots, bark,
grass and even twigs.
Every day it eats over 100 kilos
of food. That is as much food in
one day as you eat in 50 days!

Every day an elephant drinks about 240 litres of water. That is about the same as 20 full buckets.

It does not suck water through the trunk into the stomach. An elephant first fills its trunk with water, then curls the trunk round and blows the water down its throat.

The trunk can hold about one bucketful at a time.

An elephant's trunk is really a very long nose. It has many uses. It is used for collecting food which the elephant then pushes into its mouth. The trunk can pick up anything from a peanut to a very large log. It is used to smell things. It is also used to spray water over the elephant when it is bathing.

After they have had a showerbath, elephants cover themselves with mud! This is to stop insects biting them.

Elephants have the biggest teeth of all animals. The big chewing teeth inside the mouth are as big as loaves of bread. The two big teeth that grow outside the mouth are called tusks.

Tusks can grow very long.
There was once a famous elephant in Africa called Ahmed. He had tusks so long that they dragged along the ground!

A baby elephant weighs about
100 kilos when it is born. That is
about 30 times larger than you were
when you were born. The baby soon
finds its way to its mothers milk
supply between her front legs.
It drinks her milk with its mouth,
holding its trunk right back over
its head.

Elephants are wonderful mothers,
but if her baby is naughty,
she will slap it with her trunk.

Now that you have met the elephant, do you think one would be able to
walk through your front door?